Lingo Dingo
and the
Czech chef

Written by Mark Pallis
Illustrated by James Cottell

For my awesome sons- MP

For Leo and Juniper - JC

LINGO DINGO AND THE CZECH CHEF

All rights reserved. This book or any portion thereof may not be reproduced or used in any manner whatsoever without the express written permission of the publisher except for the use of brief excerpts in a review.

Story edited by Natascha Biebow, Blue Elephant Storyshaping
First Printing, 2022
ISBN: 978-1-915337-38-2
NeuWestendPress.com

Lingo Dingo
and the Czech chef

Written by Mark Pallis
Illustrated by James Cottell

NEU WESTEND PRESS

This is Lingo. She's a Dingo and she loves helping.
Anyone. Anytime. Anyhow.

Lingo often helps her stylish neighbour Gunther, who lives by himself next door. She does a few jobs and has a nice chat. It makes Gunther feel good and it makes Lingo feel good too.

One day, Lingo arranged a special birthday party for Gunther. She even ordered a cake from a famous Czech chef.

There was a knock at the door, "It must be the cake!" said Lingo. But it was a monkey.

"Dobrý den. Jmenuji se šéfkuchař Nono. Mám problém," he said.

Oh no. I can't speak Czech yet, thought Lingo. *Maybe 'Dobrý den' is like 'Hello'.*

Dobrý den = Hello; **Jmenuji se** = My name Is; **Mám problém** = I have a problem

"Dobrý den," said Lingo. Chef Nono replied slowly, "Omlouvám se. Nemohu upéct narozeninový dort."

"I don't understand," said Lingo. "But let me guess. You want…"

Omlouvám se = I am sorry; **Nemohu upéct** = I cannot bake; **narozeninový dort** = birthday cake

"Mám rozbitou troubu," explained Chef.
"Můžu použít vaši troubu?"

Chef's oven must be broken thought Lingo. "I know! Let's bake the cake together," she said.

Mám rozbitou troubu = my oven is broken;
Můžu použít vaši troubu? = can I use your oven?

Chef tapped his wrist. "Kolik je hodin? Devět hodin? Deset?" he asked.

Lingo pointed at her watch.

"Jedenáct hodin? Tak začněme! Rychle!"
They only had one hour until the party.

Kolik je hodin? = what time is it?; **Devět hodin** = nine o'clock; **Deset hodin** = ten o'clock; **Jedenáct hodin** = eleven o'clock; **Tak začněme** = let's get started; **Rychle** = quick

Chef Nono and Lingo whizzed around the kitchen:

Zástěra pro tebe = an apron for you; **Metlička** = a whisk; **Mísa na míchání** = a mixing bowl

"Podej mi máslo, cukr, vejce a mouku, prosím," said Chef.

Lingo wasn't sure what those words meant, so she just grabbed fish, coffee and onions instead.

"Rybu, kávu a cibuli. Nechutné!" laughed Chef.

Podej mi = pass me; **máslo** = butter; **cukr** = sugar; **vejce** = eggs; **mouku** = flour; **prosím** = please; **Rybu** = fish; **kávu** = coffee; **cibuli** = onions; **Nechutné** = disgusting

Chef plopped sugar, butter, eggs and flour into a bowl. "So that's what 'máslo, cukr, vejce a mouku' means!" laughed Lingo.

"Já mícham, ty mícháš, my mícháme," said Chef and together they began to mix the cake.

Já mícham = I mix; **ty mícháš** = you mix; **my mícháme** = we mix

"Konečně prášek do pečiva. Dvě lžíce," said Chef. Lingo guessed 'prášek do pečiva' meant baking powder, but how much?

Before she could ask, Chef hurried away, saying, "Promiňte, musím si odskočit."

Lingo laughed, "I can guess what 'odskočit' means!"

Konečně = finally; **prášek do pečiva** = baking powder; **Dvě lžíce** = two spoonfulls; **Promiňte** = excuse me; **musím si odskočit** = I need to do a wee wee

I wonder if this is too much? thought Lingo as she added ten spoonfulls of 'prášek do pečiva' to the mix.

She carefully put everything into the oven and before long, a sweet cakey smell filled the kitchen.

prášek do pečiva = baking powder

"Co se stalo? Je to obrovské!" said Chef.

Lingo realised she had added too much baking powder.
"Sorry," she said sheepishly.

Co se stalo? = what happened?; **Je to obrovské** = it's huge

"I know what will make you feel better," said Lingo, kindly. "Eat this 'nakladánou okurku'!"

"Hnus. Nesnáším nakládané okurky." said Chef.

They were running out of time.

Hnus = disgusting; **Nesnáším nakládané okurky** = I hate gherkins

"I've got it! Gunther loves hats, so let's turn the cakey mess into a hat cake!" said Lingo.

First she shaped the cake, then she filled balloons with icing.

Next came the best part: POP! POP! POP!

It was a messy job but in the end, the cake looked fantastic. "Červené, oranžové, žluté, zelené, modré. Fantastické," said Chef.

Červené = red; **oranžové** = orange; **žluté** = yellow; **zelené** = green; **modré** = blue; **Fantastické** = fantastic

There was a knock at the door.
"Dveře!" said Chef.
It was Gunther, and he was wearing his special hat!

"Thankyou. This makes me feel so special," said Gunther.
"You are special," replied Lingo.

Y drws = the door

Gunter was thrilled with his cake.

Chef's deep voice sang:

"Všechno nejlepší k narozeninám…"

Všechno nejlepší k narozeninám = happy birthday to you

"Foukni!" said Chef.

Gunther blew out all the candles in one puff and everyone tucked in.

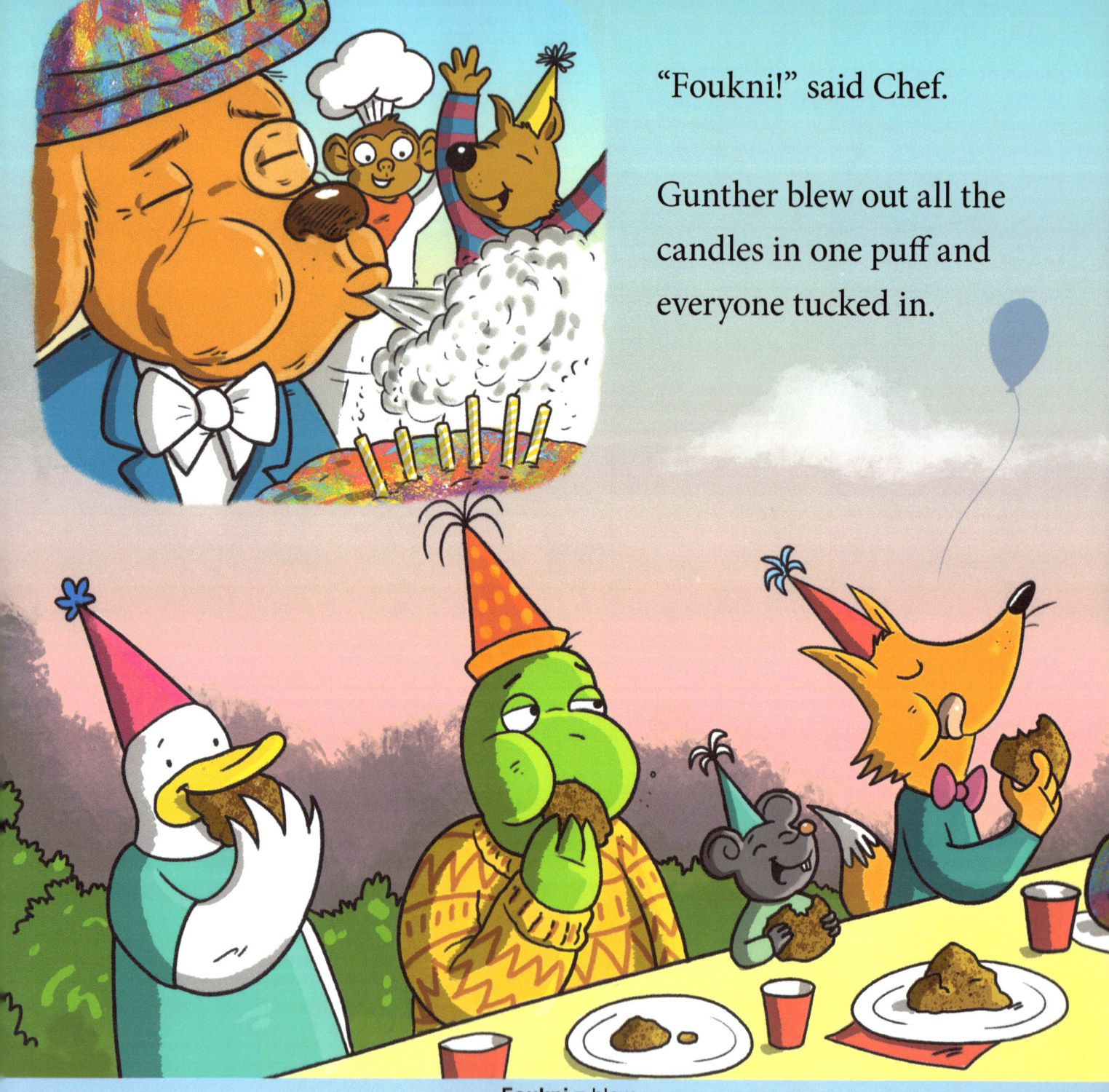

Foukni = blow

"Já jím, ty jíš, on jí, ona jí, oni jí," laughed Chef.
"My jíme!" added Lingo proudly.

Já jím = I eat; **ty jíš** = you eat; **on jí** = he eats;
ona jí = she eats; **oni jí** = they eat; **my jíme** = we eat

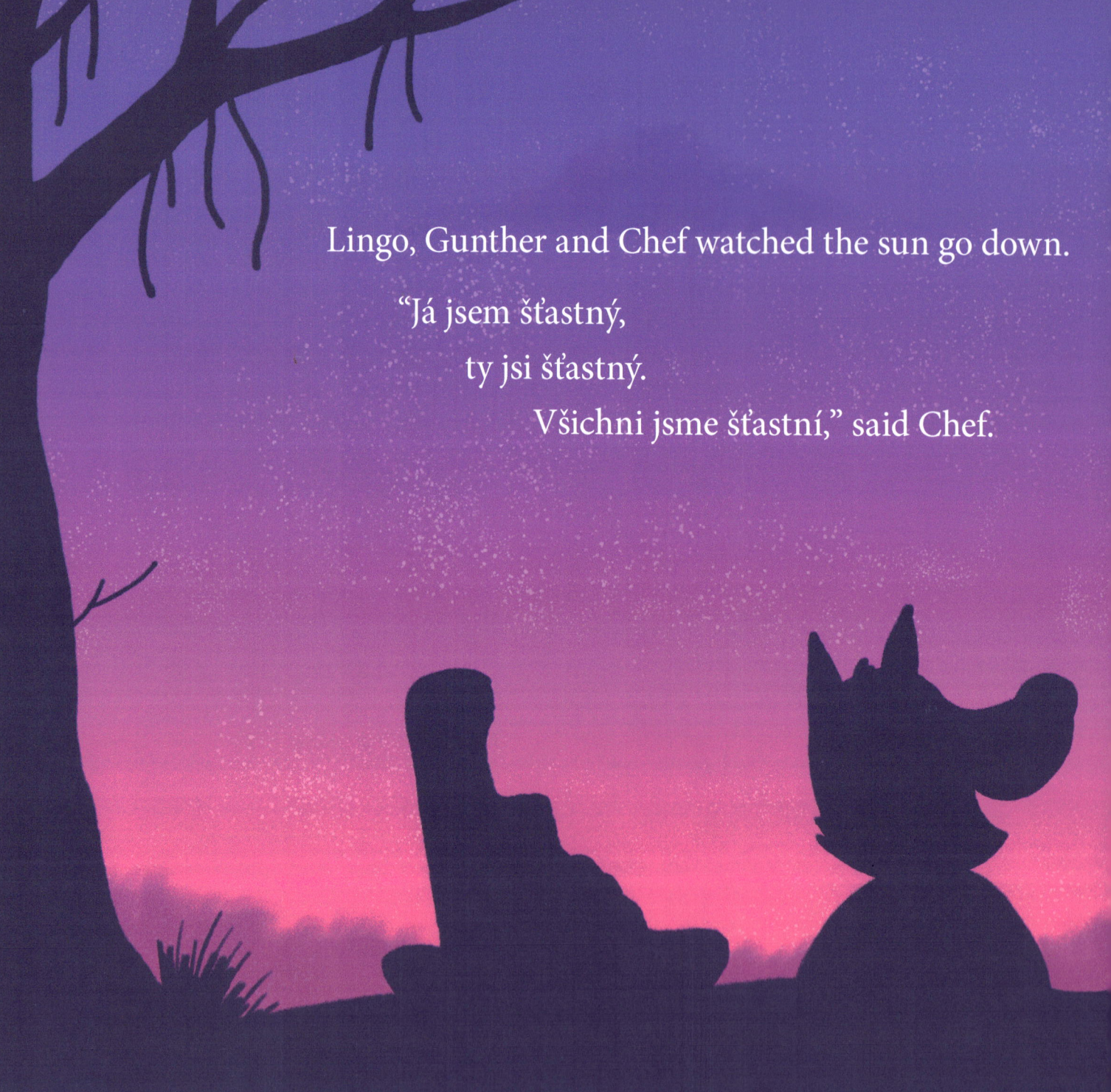

Lingo, Gunther and Chef watched the sun go down.

"Já jsem šťastný,

ty jsi šťastný.

Všichni jsme šťastní," said Chef.

Já jsem šťastný = I am happy; **ty jsi šťastný** = you are happy; **Všichni jsme šťastní** = we are all happy

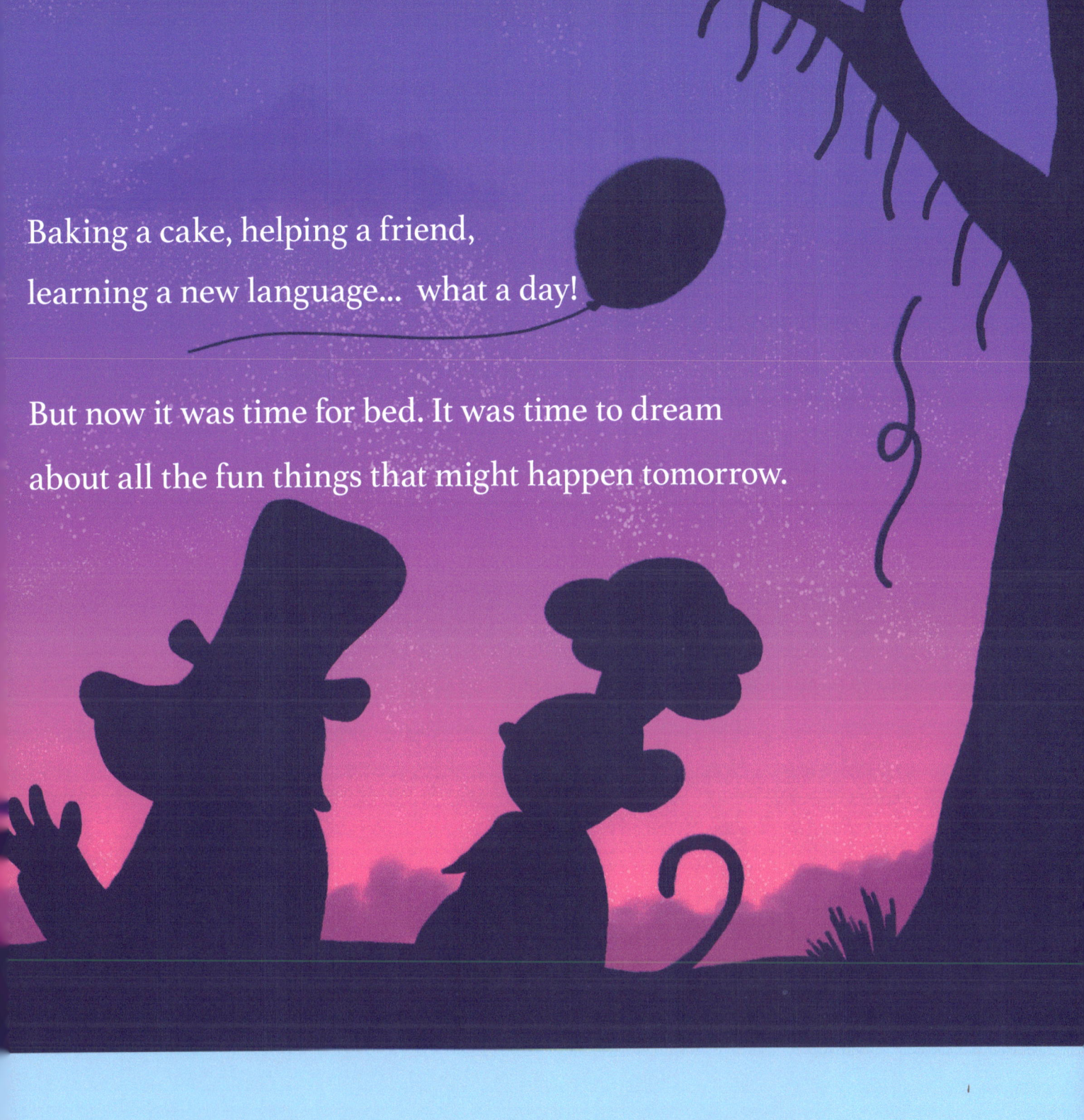

Baking a cake, helping a friend, learning a new language... what a day!

But now it was time for bed. It was time to dream about all the fun things that might happen tomorrow.

Learning to love languages

An additional language opens a child's mind, broadens their horizons and enriches their emotional life. Research has shown that the time between a child's birth and their sixth or seventh birthday is a "golden period" when they are most receptive to new languages. This is because they have an in-built ability to distinguish the sounds they hear and make sense of them. The Story-powered Language Learning Method taps into these natural abilities.

How the Story-powered language learning Method works

We create an emotionally engaging and funny story for children and adults to enjoy together, just like any other picture book. Studies show that social interaction, like enjoying a book together, is critical in language learning.

Through the story, we introduce a relatable character who speaks only in the new language. This helps build empathy and a positive attitude towards people who speak different languages. These are both important aspects in laying the foundations for lasting language acquisition in a child's life.

As the story progresses, the child naturally works with the characters to discover the meanings of a wide range of fun new words. Strategic use of humour ensures that this subconscious learning is rewarded with laughter; the child feels good and the first seeds of a lifelong love of languages are sown.

For more information and free learning resources visit www.neuwestendpress.com

You can learn more words and phrases with these hilarious, heartwarming stories from NEU WESTEND PRESS

Available in over 50 different languages!

@MARK_PALLIS on twitter
www.neuwestendpress.com

To download your FREE certifcate, and more cool stuff, visit
www.neuwestendpress.com

@jamescottell on INSTAGRAM
www.jamescottellstudios.co.uk

"I want people to be so busy laughing, they don't realise they're learning!"
Mark Pallis

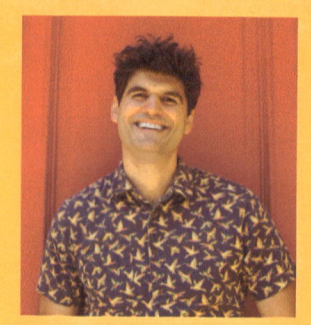

Crab and Whale is the bestselling story of how a little Crab helps a big Whale. It's carefully designed to help even the most energetic children find a moment of calm and focus. It also includes a special mindful breathing exercise and affirmation for children. Also available in French as 'Crabe et Baleine.'

Featured as one of Mindful.org's 'Seven Mindful Children's books'

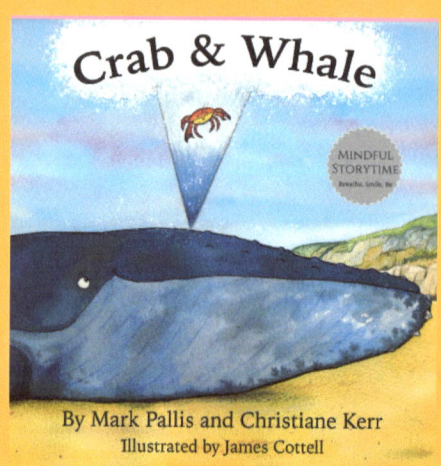

Do you call them hugs or cuddles?

In this funny, heartwarming story, you will laugh out loud as two loveable gibbons try to figure out if a hug is better than a cuddle and, in the process, learn how to get along.

A perfect story for anyone who loves a hug (or a cuddle!)

www.markpallis.com

www.ingramcontent.com/pod-product-compliance
Lightning Source LLC
Chambersburg PA
CBHW040021130526
44590CB00036B/42